NORTH LIGHT

NORTH LIGHT

Ari Trausti Guðmundsson
Ragnar Th. Sigurðsson

Iceland
Review

The ice-covered Lake Kleifarvatn (SW Iceland) on a frosty winter's morning. There is more than enough room for a few lonely skaters.

Contents

I   INTRODUCTION 9

II   THE BRIGHT NIGHT 13
At the Arctic Circle
Short Summer Nights, Cool Weather

III   THE HEART OF LIGHT 23
A Wandering Star
The Elusive Daylight

IV   THE LONGEST NIGHT 33
Seasons to Taste
Long Winter Nights, Cool Weather

V   GLITTERING ICE AND SNOW 45
Cold Companions
Glaciers and Ice Caps

VI   ILLUMINATED SKY 55
The Northern Lights – Why?

VII COLOURS IN THE SKY 63
Heavenly Arches and Circles

VIII WARM ICELAND 71
Light and Energy

IX   FIRE FROM WITHIN 77
Zones and Systems
Born and Bred by Fire

X   JUST WAIT AND SEE 85
The Sea is the Key

Introduction

It's a late-April Thursday in Reykjavík, the capital of Iceland. There's no morning rush-hour traffic and most shops are closed. It's not close to Easter and it's not Independence Day either. So what's going on? The answer is simple, but unique. You see, in Iceland, most employees, pupils and students take a day off each year on the first Thursday after April 18. And this particular day is an official holiday. The mood of a good Sunday fills the air and society runs at half speed or less. Brass bands are on the move in urban areas, festivities add light to the day and children in pageants flock to vantage points to see the celebrations. In the evening, cafés, bars, restaurants and discos flood with people. Iceland is probably the only country in the industrialised world where you can take in all this – on this particular day.

Why all the merriment? Well, it's the First Day of Summer! It's hardly "true" summer in the usual meaning of the word. In reality, Iceland is only beginning to see spring at this time of year. In fact, the true month of spring and revival is May. However, in the old Icelandic almanac, the main unit for measuring time was the seven-day week, not the month. In the past, people used to divide

■ Migratory birds, like these Greylag geese, are among the first signs of spring (Kópavogur, SW Iceland).

9

the year into two 26-week periods: winter and summer. They would use phrases such as, "I'll be there on Friday in the fourth week of winter" or "on Thursday in the 20th week of summer".

According to the old almanac, the half-year-long term of summer began in late April, about one month after the equinox. This would be a day full of promise in Iceland. At this time of the year in the northern hemisphere, days slowly become longer, the temperature creeps gradually above freezing and the first migratory birds have already greeted the sun-hungry Icelanders. These ever-returning events mean prosperous growth, vigorous work, better weather and a closeness to nature that is softer and very different from that experienced in its wintry mood. The term "First Day of Summer" embraces and airs these promises. The reason for celebrating the season of light in the high north is evident.

There is, however, more to the celebration of light than festivities on the eve of spring. Light in the Arctic is a universal gift to the senses. Light illuminates nature. Light means life.

Nature is a magnificent artist. It sculpts forms beyond the imagination and paints more varied shades of colour than any human artist. In Iceland, the artistic views in nature never cease to create a sense of wonderment and inspiration. Despite Iceland's relatively modest size of 103,000 square kilometres, this country displays a multitude of changing, splendid exhibitions of nature's artistic skills. Icelandic nature is a veritable chameleon.

While the human artist tries to capture the mood of his motif for posterity, blend in his own feelings and purposefully evoke thoughts within the viewer, nature is a blind artist of the very moment; within seconds the environment may change and new vistas greet the eye. The only way to capture nature as it flatters each second is to rely on a still camera – freezing the immaculate view onto paper – stopping time. A photographer's mission is to display that very image of still time. An author of words only speaks to the imagination.

The magic of the moment in Icelandic nature has to do with the restless display of light. The weather changes abruptly and Iceland's bright summer nights, as well as the prevailing darkness of winter, have always fascinated photographers. Winter snows and thick sheets of ice may serve up views that are completely different than those seen from the same vantage point in summer. Icelandic nature is a master of disguise.

The vast open space of Iceland dwarfs high mountains as well as wide lava flows. It even diminishes large ice caps. The pervasive stillness reveals nothing of the latent, internal forces of the earth that are so often on the loose. Iceland is, however, far from being devoid of life. Even though the birch may seem somewhat timid and grass slopes may cling precariously beneath high cliffs, Iceland supports vigorous ecosystems. The Icelanders themselves have managed to sculpt their own landscape in towns and farms and illuminate nature by harnessing clean energy. They still live partly as hunters, but in a modern way.

Their task for this millennium is to preserve nature as the artist it is, while living off nature in a sustainable way, in harmony with its capacity and virtues. The purpose of this book is to point out some of the reasons for doing so, as well as to show why light in the North will always be a reason for celebration and wonder.

Let's coin the phrase "North Light".

Geothermal fumes lend an eerie air to the glaciated Kerlingarfjöll mountains (central Iceland). ■

The Bright Night

Night and day are equally long in late March. A few weeks farther into the bright season, life in Iceland responds and the classic signs of spring become evident. The snow melts. Thaws swell brooks and rivers while the first vague, green hues adorn April's vegetation. Now, the day stretches far into the former winter night. Daylight greets people on their way to work. At night, though, the temperature may still sink below freezing. If northerly winds gain strength in early May, daytime temperatures may even drop well below freezing – a true reminder of your whereabouts. Occasional snow showers may linger into June.

New, small and fine-smelling leaves of birch are regarded as a tell-tale sign of spring. Only 1.5% of Iceland has tree-cover. Small native birch forests display their verdure in early June. In addition, imported species such as spruce, pine and aspen are widespread and constitute larger, commercial forests or provide shade in urban gardens. The woods come to life in May and June and draw more people to nature. A surprising number of private gardens are found in Iceland. In fact, most households have one. Thousands upon thousands of Icelanders take to gardening and house-maintenance as soon as thaws relieve the soil of its internal ice layer. There is no permafrost in lowland soil but a late winter ice-layer might be 20–50 cm thick in the soil of an Icelandic garden. The intra-soil ice vanishes in a matter of weeks as soon as the temperature hovers above freezing.

The first migratory bird to appear in early March is the swift, agile and often aggressive Arctic skua. Other species follow in April. The most celebrated visitors, however, find their way across the North Atlantic in late April and early May. These are the golden plover and the Arctic tern. Both make news headlines each year – definite proof of spring! These birds arrive in small, unobtrusive groups and disperse over the whole country. Seaside cliffs hold more spectacular sights. Millions of sea birds precariously inhabit the lava and tuff

■ A solitary puffin watches over the midnight sun from the island of Drangey (N Iceland).

Reykjavík's neighbouring towns of Kópavogur and Hafnarfjörður seen from the capital on an August night.

precipices. A cacophony of shrieking, croaking and whistling fills the air and airborne traffic is incredibly dense. The Icelandic stock of puffins alone contains more than four million individuals. These small birds are like the majority of their Icelandic human counterparts – stoical but busy.

Boat and trawler traffic intensifies in the spring and early summer when the sea is somewhat calmer and many fish species flock toward the coastline. Different industries on land become free of darkness or snow and, suddenly, builders, road crews and farmers are at their busiest. Domestic animals are set free from their pens and houses. A large stock of sheep now grows even larger and the woolly parents and lambs will start roaming the highlands as soon as the vegetation allows grazing. Riders greet the spring on horseback. Anglers dust off their fishing gear. Brisk trout and salmon flock into Iceland's rivers, aptly famous for their fine but somewhat elusive catches.

In towns, life becomes busier than ever as well. But you also notice that life has taken on a leisurely tint – especially on sunny days, which appear too rarely at times. People tend to savour the sunlight everywhere they can, even if the temperature may be barely high enough for anyone to sit or lie comfortably outdoors. The usual summertime temperature in Iceland is between 10° and 20°C. Over 20°C? Well, that's a heat wave!

Children are another characteristic feature of the Icelandic landscape. There seem to be so many of them, playing or helping out at the workplace in towns and on farms throughout the bright summer. But the explanation for there being so many children around is not to be found in some extraordinary Icelandic fertility. Rather, for decades now, schools in Iceland have simply closed down from late May to early September. In most countries, the school summer holiday is much shorter. Icelanders compensate by having longer school hours each school day during the winter. However, the total number of school days in the year is somewhat lower than in many other countries.

Fine geothermally heated pools and health centres fill to the brim with sun-starved people – that is, those who have not already ven-

AT THE ARCTIC CIRCLE

Situated roughly between 64 and 67 degrees northern latitude (67°N), Iceland actually touches the Arctic Circle. As we mentioned before, the country's total land area is 103,000 sq km (approx. 300 by 330 km). The total sea area within the 200-nautical-mile fishing limit is 758,000 sq km. Only 1% of Iceland is cultivated; 25–30% is covered by vegetation, 3% by lakes, 11% by recent lava flows and 12% by glacier ice. Greenland is only 287 km away, the Faroe Islands 420 km, Scotland 780 km and Norway 970 km. In 2001 the Icelandic population was close to 290,000 with a life expectancy of 77 years for males and 81 years for females, both being among the highest in the world. The population has increased by 0.9–1.3% per year for the past few years. In 2000, the GDP (GNP) per capita was USD 30,597 – the eighth highest in the world. Marine products accounted for 63.3% of the total (2000).

Around summer solstice, the late evening sun can make you do strange things. ■

A glimpse of Arctic summer in Iceland. Eider ducks and icebergs at Jökulsárlón glacial lagoon (SE Iceland).

tured for a few weeks to the Mediterranean countries, so popular among Nordic people. In the Mediterranean, you can rely on the sun. But in Iceland, you just never know. In Iceland's "Northern Capital" of Akureyri, southerly winds in July might, for example, boost temperatures to 25°C one day while the next day's strong northern wind may make thermometers plummet to 3°C.

The bright summers of Iceland add new dimensions to both the landscape and human activities. Pastel colours and ever-changing shadows combined with clear air often create a fairy-tale environment. A calm, bright night has almost intoxicating effects on many people. In general, Icelanders tend to be more active and sleep less in summer than winter. Most visitors are no more immune to this lure of the North than the Icelanders are.

Summer solstice is on June 22. In Reykjavík, the sun looms above the horizon for a good 22 hours and then barely sets. Akureyri has almost 24 hours of brightness, providing for midnight-sun golf (with black golf balls, they say). On the Icelandic island of Grímsey at the Arctic Circle, and at the fringes of the Melrakkaslétta peninsula, true midnight sun draws people to enjoy a remarkable vista on a clear night. Icelanders celebrate *Jónsmessunótt*, the evening of June 23 (Midsummer's Eve). Bonfires and feasts are common and, according to folklore, eerie incidents do occur on that particular night. Those in dire need of having all their wishes come true can, for example, seek out certain lakes and tarns where wishing stones float into view at midnight.

By late August, the night is already needlessly long and the first signs of autumn appear: scant northern lights, red leaves and frozen morning dew.

SHORT SUMMER NIGHTS, COOL WEATHER

From early May to early August, Icelanders cherish their long hours of brightness. From early June to late July, they see practically no darkness at all, or just a few hours at most as July passes. Around June 23, there are 24 hours of daylight. This annual extended period of daylight shifts Iceland's weather from cool, overcast days (often with rain) to warmer, sunny days with temperatures varying between 8° and 25°C. The average lowlands July temperature is about 11°C in the south (which has more annual precipitation) and 10°C in the north (which has less annual precipitation). A prominent föhn-effect prevails in Iceland. During a typical period of föhn, southerly winds bring precipitation to the southern part of the country. Meanwhile, the air dries out in the central highlands and descends – drier and warmer – into the north. Recorded temperature highs vary from 20°C to 30°C. A reverse scenario applies to cold, moist air, borne as wind from the north, albeit somewhat cooler. And the same process is at work for western or eastern winds.

The late evening sun lights up Reykjavík city centre. ∎

The Heart of Light

Our sun is a cherished source of life but its nuclear furnace emits not only benevolent light and warmth but deadly radiation as well. Fortunately, the earth's atmosphere helps to protect life from the sun's harmful emissions. This same atmosphere can cause the sun to appear as a beautiful yellow ball and the sky as a bottomless bowl of equally beautiful light-blue water.

The sun has always been a timekeeper. Not only the heart of light to our eyes, it is equally the heart of time. By observing the rhythm of sunrise and sunset along with the sun's varying height above the horizon, people in the past could crudely keep track of time. As man ventured far out to sea in search of land, fame and fortune, the sun became a marker.

All that, plus the evident influence of the sun on all living beings, has lent it an aura of benevolence, even deity. The regular features

■ Neither the rays of the winter sun nor the earth's internal heat can melt the ice at Krýsuvík (SW Iceland).

■ Sunset at Svínafell near the Skaftafell national park (SE Iceland).

of the sun's movements, even the sun's very existence, have been celebrated in almost all cultures on earth at one time or another. The day after winter solstice, *jól* or *jóladagur* in Icelandic (*juletiden* in other Scandinavian languages and "Yule" in English), has always been the most prominent of feasts and holidays in Iceland. Before the adoption of Christianity in Iceland in 1000, *jól* was celebrated as a feast of light, and afterwards as Christmas. Another celebration, *Jónsmessunótt* (*St. Hans Aften* in other Scandinavian languages, "Midsummer's Eve" in English), was held after summer solstice in the wonderful, almost unearthly light of the midnight sun. After the adoption of Christianity, the tradition lingered on and is still celebrated in the Nordic countries, including Iceland.

True midnight sun in the north is seen within the Arctic Circle – the area north of the 66.33 parallel. There, the sun simply doesn't dis-appear below the horizon regardless of the hour. This, of course, happens in the period around summer solstice. And the further north you venture, the longer the period of a non-setting sun.

The midnight sun is deeply red. A large part of the sky around the sun lights up, blazing with colours ranging from red and yellow to purple and deep blue. The reason for the red colour, indeed for the entire colour display, lies in the atmosphere: when the sun is low in the sky, close to the horizon, its light-rays have to travel through denser air than when the sun is shining from high above. The densest part of the atmosphere is the 5–10 km layer of air closest to earth. Dense air means stronger refraction (bending) of light than thin air does. Thus, more of the reddish colours appear to the eye. The surface of the sea adds still another dimension to the spectacular midnight sun on a clear, calm night. The sun and its light reflect

A WANDERING STAR

Our sun is a medium-sized, energy-generating, gas sun star chiefly composed of hydrogen and helium. The core temperature, where nuclear fusion is at work, is at least 12,000,000˚C but the surface temperature is close to "only" 6,000˚C. The size of the sun is enormous (1,500,000 km in diameter). If the earth were placed at the centre, our moon would be halfway between the core and the surface. The average distance from the earth to the sun is 150,000,000 km. The sun emits all sorts of electromagnetic waves, including ultraviolet light, visible light and also heat in the form of infrared light. The sun rotates slowly around its axis and travels along with the whole solar system in a circle around the centre of the Milky Way Galaxy. The apparent movement of the sun as it rises in the east and sets in the west is a result of the earth's counter-clockwise rotation around its own axis. As the earth also rotates around the sun – approximately every 365 days – the location of the sun's highest point in the heavens each day progresses slowly across the sky. The sun has been around for some 4–5 billion years and it will stay around for another 4–5 billion. Then, it will expand, cool, contract and partly blow up. Its remains will become a small, dense "hot dwarf sun", unable to sustain life further in its solar system.

Buttercups seen through a veil of spray from a waterfall. ■

■ The parish church, educational and research centre of Reykholt (W Iceland) in the chill of midwinter.

off the ocean, and sea lustres range from almost black and silver to orange and gold. If any part of the land is covered with snow or the sea is covered with pack ice, their white surfaces become pink and violet. Glaciated mountains and ice caps seem to merge with the lower part of the sky; quite unlike the sight when the common "Alpine glow" decorates high, ice-clad mountains at lower latitudes. In the high north, a thin greenish stripe may appear momentarily between the white surface and the sky. In a similar occurrence, there's sometimes a green flash when the sun touches the horizon of the sea.

THE ELUSIVE DAYLIGHT

For those unfamiliar with the true movements of the earth and the sun, the sun's journey across the sky each day and all the variations in its course must have been confusing. After all, it seems as if the sun rotates around the earth. The picture becomes further complicated because the earth's axis tilts a good 23 degrees from a level extended from the sun's equator. That's why we have seasons and varying lengths of day and night. Day and night are the results of our globe's spinning. It always hides half of itself – "the dark side" – from the sunlight at any given time. In winter, when the northern half of the earth leans away from the sun, the glowing star appears much lower in the sky in that particular hemisphere (and the night gets longer). Then, as the earth leans toward the sun in summer, the days become longer and the sun rises higher in the sky. At the North Pole, there is one dark period with no sun appearing above the horizon for some six months. For the next six months, a low but glaring 24-hour-per-day sun completely illuminates the sky and the earth below. Meanwhile, at the equator, night and day are almost equally long the whole year round and the sun is high above one's head at noon. Anywhere in-between the North Pole and the equator, the bright hours are somewhat longer in the summer and shorter in the winter. In Reykjavík, a very long period of light precedes summer solstice and lingers afterward – about two months altogether. Around summer solstice, the sun is up almost 24 hours a day; but this only lasts for a few days. In mid-winter, the sun stays above the horizon only for some 3.5 to 6 hours per day.

A small patch of vegetation adds a touch of life to an otherwise harsh landscape (near Kóngsfell, SW Iceland). ■

The Longest Night

Night and day are equally long worldwide in late September. By that time in Iceland signs of autumn are evident: nights with below-freezing temperatures; falling leaves; migratory birds leaving the country. These telltale occurrences remind Icelanders that from then on, darkness is slowly but surely creeping upon them and their homesteads.

Iceland's main month of autumn is October. The weather is slowly deteriorating. High winds arrive more frequently and precipitation tends to increase. The first light snows have already whitened the highland mountains. Most industries simply adjust to the changing environment. Indoor activity is much less affected, of course, and many of the larger companies go on with business as if nothing were happening. But in more traditional occupations, autumn indeed means change. Farmers have to round up hundreds of thou-

■ A November view of the Öxarárfoss waterfall at Þingvellir, where huge chasms illustrate tectonic-plate spreading in Iceland (SW Iceland).

■ Geothermal fumes and northern lights at Svartsengi (SW Iceland). The Illahraun lava field dates back to the 13th century.

sands of sheep. The surefooted Icelandic horse still comes in handy during the roundup of both sheep and semi-wild horses in late September and early October. Smaller fishing vessels cease activity and tie up in the harbour. Students return to school in early September and, suddenly, urban life is busier than it has been; traffic, shopping and social activities all pick up their pace.

So do many other activities, especially the arts and indoor hobbies. During the first two to three weeks of October, dozens of fresh plays, operas, concerts, exhibitions and things of the like highlight each week in the City of Reykjavík and in "large" towns. Publishers suddenly become busy and about 500 new Icelandic book titles will appear during the winter months for Iceland's book-hungry population, which leads the world in literacy. Dozens upon dozens of new CDs will be released. This somewhat strange seasonal norm for activity in Iceland is not only reflected in cultural offerings but in ordinary work as well. Furthermore, the sheer number of artistic and other cultural contributions is staggering when you consider

Iceland's small population. A countermeasure against the creeping darkness? Why not?

In December, the weather goes into a rather harsh mode. Very cold weather with temperatures below -15° or -20°C is uncommon in the lowlands. Even so, frequent high winds can make 0° to -10°C bitterly cold. The precipitation lands mostly as snow in the north, but little snow usually falls in the south until late December. In the south, it rains from time to time through the whole winter. Alternating thaws and periods of freezing temperatures put a strain on people and vegetation alike – and, of course, on roads and buildings too. Luckily, Icelanders know how to make full use of their wealth of geothermal energy. About 90% of all homes in Iceland are heated geothermally. Iceland's numerous outdoor swimming pools don't close in the winter and people flock to them to indulge in their soothing, exquisite water and to socialise. Swimming lessons are compulsory in all lower grade schools and pools brim with noisy, active children during certain hours.

SEASONS TO TASTE

Unlike some of the planets in our solar system, the earth has a tilting axis of rotation. It is tilted 23.5 degrees in relation to a plane that extends from the sun's equator. The earth moves at an incredible speed of 90,000 km per hour in its elliptical orbit around the sun. The envelope of air surrounding the globe moves along with the planet so we feel no rush. The earth completes one orbit in a little over 365 days. The northern hemisphere tilts toward the sun for about half the journey (late March to late September) when we experience the warmer and brighter part of the year ("summer"). At the North Pole during these same six months, there is only daylight (or "summer"). Meanwhile, at the equator there is little change in season. Those of us in-between live through spring, summer and early autumn during that six-month period. At the same time (late March to late September), the southern hemisphere is tilting away from the sun. People "down under" (between the South Pole and the equator) are experiencing late autumn, winter and early spring. The northern part of the globe tilts away from the sun from late September to late March and we now go through our colder, darker season ("winter"). Total darkness and winter grip the North Pole. The northernmost towns of the world are located between 64 and 78 degrees north where the dark hours of winter are far longer than in the densely inhabited lands further south.

A winter super-jeep expedition in an ice canyon on the edge of the Dyngjujökull outlet glacier (Vatnajökull ice cap). ■

In late December (winter solstice being on December 22), daylight or sunlight sneaks over Iceland for only 3–4 hours. Many people feel somewhat depressed by all the darkness, but surveys have nevertheless revealed that fewer Icelanders have problems enduring darkness than most other dwellers of the high north.

In winter, snow and ice envelop the highlands. Snow cover may vary from one winter to another. Commonly, it attains 1–4 m in depth but in some sheltered areas, little snow may fall for months. High up on the Vatnajökull ice cap, some 10–14 m of snow comes down in eight to nine months. These highland areas are playgrounds for skiers, skidoos and specially converted super-jeeps with oversized tyres. By letting most of the air out of the tyres, drivers can make their vehicles "float" on any kind of snow. Long distances may be covered in a few hours, be they high up on one of the ice caps or on remote snow-covered heaths. Ice climbers make their daring moves while Alpine and Nordic skiers have ample opportunities to pursue their sports not far from many Icelandic towns, including Reykjavík. The Arctic darkness and often-tough conditions challenge outdoor types looking for a winter adventure in Iceland.

In the highlands as well as in lowlands – away from illuminated towns – the aurora borealis appears readily and blazes throughout the sky in a spectacular play of nature. The silent symphony of starlight, moonlight and northern lights is both intriguing and beautiful. Iceland is an ideal place to observe the aurora borealis.

Three prominent feasts and holidays illuminate the dark period from December to February. These are Christmas, New Year's Eve and Þorrablót, an ancient Nordic feast probably held in honour of

Reykjavík on a windy day in the depths of winter. ∎

■ Despite temperatures below -15 to -20°C, spring-fed rivers tend not to freeze over (at Húsafell, SW Iceland).

Thor (Þór) and named after the month of Þorri (a pre-Christian name). Icelanders celebrate Christmas from December 24 to 26. The preparations start early and involve extensive shopping and planning. Unusual lighting and a flood of books typify Icelandic Christmas celebrations. Coloured lights decorate most homes, including small and large apartment houses. In more windows than not, small coloured lights or candelabras of seven white lights illuminate the winter night. Again, Christmas is the book and CD season. Hundreds of thousands of books become presents, making the book the most common of all Christmas gifts. It has historically been the Icelander's omnipresent companion, tailor-made for seemingly countless hours of Arctic darkness.

When it comes to New Year's Eve, two special things catch the eye: fireworks and bonfires (brenna, pl. brennur). The fireworks are not municipal. But they are more elaborate and extensive than in any other place in the world. Almost every household buys large quantities of assorted fireworks, often from rescue teams and sports clubs selling fireworks to help finance their work. By midnight in

larger towns, the sky glows panoramically from thousands upon thousands of firework displays. Before midnight, grown-ups and children alike attend a nearby brenna. Songs, fireworks and festive crowds make such bonfires well worth a visit.

According to the old almanac, late January (between 19 and 25) beholds the start of the month of Þorri (pronounced "thorri"). The ancestors of the modern Icelanders celebrated this roughly four-week period with heavy eating and stout drinking during successive feasts. The food included different courses of sheep intestines, smoked lamb, whale blubber, singed sheep heads, dried fish, milk curd called skyr, and fermented shark. Most of the meaty dishes were preserved in whey. The modern feast (still called Þorrablót) continues to offer the old dishes, some a bit modified but still original. Drinks consist of sodas, beer and the Icelandic brennivín schnapps. It is customary today for most companies, associations and institutions to hold a Þorrablót for their employees.

LONG WINTER NIGHTS, COOL WEATHER

From late October to late February in Iceland, the long hours of darkness are manifest. From late November to late January, there are few hours of brightness. On December 22, the sun rises above the horizon for only about four hours. The further north you venture, the shorter the day, of course. Winter weather in the south is rather mild. Sunny, clear days with temperatures not far below freezing alternate with rainy days, snowstorms and days with overcast skies, with temperatures around freezing. Very low temperatures are rare. The weather is cooler in the north, with more snow and more frequent below-freezing days. Rainy days are rare in the north and so are temperatures below -15° to -20°C. The average January temperature in the lowland regions is about 0°C in the south (with more annual precipitation) and -2°C in the north (with less annual precipitation). The föhn-effect still exists in winter, but to a lesser degree than in the summer.

Newly formed pancake ice in Sauðárkrókur harbour (N Iceland). ■

Glittering Ice and Snow

Despite Iceland's name, the area covered by perpetual ice, some 11,000–12,000 sq km, is only about one third of the area covered by different types of green vegetation. Common sense tells us that the name "Greenland" would consequently be more appropriate than "Iceland". But the name "Greenland" is already used for another country with almost 90% of its land area covered by ice and snow all year long – a true "ice land"! The glacier cover in Iceland is much smaller. Gleaming white patches on satellite photos show the true size of the ice fields. In mid-winter, however, most of Iceland is white from a bird's-eye view. Snows cover most highland areas and, at times, a large part of the lowlands as well.

The winter snows and the white uppermost snow layers on the glaciers create a special kind of light or, more precisely, many different hues and colours. Clean snow reflects 80–90% of the light it

■ Ice caves in glaciers are commonly channels for meltwater and can only be entered in winter (Vatnajökull ice cap).

■ Super-jeeps cross the remote snow-clad surface of the Brúarjökull outlet glacier, southwest of Mt. Snæfell, an extinct volcano (E Iceland).

receives. Therefore, the snow cover produces sharp shades – especially shades of blue – during the day because the sun is never high in the sky during the winter. If the sun is close to the horizon in the morning or in the evening, the light becomes deeper in colour. Immediately after sunset, the sky and the snow take on an increasingly violet colour. Before sunrise, a growing yellowish-bluish hue lights up the eastern sky close to the horizon. Complimenting this immensely beautiful play of light, the Arctic air is commonly quite crisp and clean. Visibility is often excellent and all landscape contours become sharp. In very cold and calm weather, however, a frosty haze may appear, especially in areas with somewhat moist air. Different kinds of rime, hoar frost and snow crystals can, under the right circumstances, reflect sunlight – causing the rime or snow surface to sparkle like tiny diamonds.

Ice both reflects and refracts (bends) light. Ice contains air bubbles and impurities that influence to what degree light is affected. Exposed to sunlight or slight heat, ice quickly becomes opaque or white. The result of these different factors is an array of colours in the ice. Also influencing ice colours are the angle and colour of incoming sunlight. These colours may range from light blue, through the darker blue shades to blue-green and dark green, in addition to white and grey. Imagine North Light displayed under the midnight sun on a crevassed glacier. Or in the morning among floating icebergs! "Out of this world," an intrepid explorer once said.

In the late mornings and early evenings of winter, only faint light illuminates the sky. This particular light has an unusual look to it. It is twilight and it makes snowy countryside vistas look like porcelain landscapes. A clear winter night with moonshine, starlight, the northern lights and reflections from a glittering, white surface can have an eerie effect. The night can be so bright that you need no extra light to find your way around.

Cold Companions

In Iceland, most of the snow that falls in the winter melts during the summer. What remains in the glaciated areas turns – by metamorphic processes – into compacted snow (firn) and later into glacier ice. This leftover snow enters the ice depths of the thick glaciers and will, much later on, return to the sea and air as water or water vapour when the ice melts below the snow line. There are five types of ice found in Iceland: 1) glacier ice, 2) ice made of frozen water on lakes and rivers, 3) atmospheric ice (microscopic flying ice crystals), 4) pack-ice made of frozen sea water, and 5) interstitial ice in the topsoil. For six to nine months of the Icelandic year, the majority of all precipitation falls as snow.

Iceland's highest summit, Hvannadalshnúkur (2,119 m), rises up from the rim of the Öræfajökull volcano (SE Iceland). ∎

■ Members of the Iceland Glaciological Society in the volcanic vent of the 1998 Grímsvötn eruption (Vatnajökull ice cap).

Winter travel in the Icelandic highlands is common. People often use skis or skidoos, but the most popular mode of travel is the super-jeep. Inland sands and lava fields are tough terrains to cross. Ice-cap crossing can be even more arduous because of low temperatures (-20° to -30°C) and high winds. However, the payoff for such an outing is a series of magnificent views like those found in Greenland or Antarctica when fairly close to the Polar Circles. The sheer size of the highlands makes them less crowded than most similar areas. You may have an area the size of a huge city just for yourself.

In towns, ice and snow often annoy people. Traffic in the towns of the northwest, north and northeast commonly becomes very slow or even comes to a complete standstill. Icy roads prove hazardous to drivers all over Iceland. In the southwest, south and southeast, heavy snows in towns are somewhat rarer than in other parts of the country but are still a problem at times. In any case, snowy towns keep children happy and snow-covered urban areas can often be beautiful on clear, sunny days.

GLACIERS AND ICE CAPS

The largest ice fields in Iceland are termed "ice caps". An ice cap is a thick sheet of ice covering a large area where only the highest mountain summits protrude through the ice. Icelandic ice caps range in size from 160 to 8,300 sq km. They are 200–900 m thick. A few small ice caps rest on large, single mountains. Outlet glaciers flow in different directions from the main ice mass of each ice cap. More than 20 outlet glaciers flow from the Vatnajökull ice cap alone. Relatively fast-flowing, alpine glaciers cover high, steep mountains – most of which are volcanoes. If a volcanic eruption occurs beneath an ice cap or in a glaciated volcano, huge floods may sweep adjacent regions. In 1996, one such "glacier burst" followed a sub-glacial eruption in Vatnajökull. The discharge was 50,000 cu m of water per second (about 12,000 gallons) and over 3 billion tons of water rushed to the sea. That amounts to 3,000 billion litres or 750 billion gallons!

Frozen autumn dew. ∎

VI

Illuminated Sky

Black sky, dancing lights of yellow, green and violet… white, glittering snow, pierced by a few icebergs; this is the classic (or stereotypical, if you will) view of the High Arctic. A true image, yes, but not so easy to witness as you may think. Sombre, overcast skies and too much man-made light are two reasons for not being able to spot the northern lights (aurora borealis) at any given time or place in Iceland during the winter. Common street lighting simply overrides the rather faint illumination from the northern lights. Another reason lies within the sun's activity. The northern lights are associated with a flow of charged atomic particles, electrons amongst them, from the sun to earth. The intensity of the particle flow varies over time. Consequently, the occurrence and intensity of the northern lights vary over time as well. Many days may elapse without any noticeable trace of northern lights in the sky above Iceland. Then,

■ The northern lights often crown the skies over Iceland.

following such a period, the sky may flicker night after night with this beautiful phenomenon, for hours and hours at a time.

In olden times, people didn't know why the northern lights occurred or even what they really were. In Icelandic folklore, it is said that if a pregnant woman stares at the northern lights, her child will be born blind. We now know that the northern lights occur in the earth's ionosphere, commonly at an altitude of 100–150 km, and that they can be likened to the light emitted from a fluorescent light tube. The northern lights sparkle all around the globe throughout the year but their intensity is highest and their altitude lowest in a zone that stretches around the northern hemisphere between 60 and 80 degrees of latitude (60°N–80°N), and similarly in the southern hemisphere. So, Iceland and other countries some 2,000–3,000 km away from the poles are perfect places to see or study the northern lights. The lights either appear as long, moving curtains of light or flow like radiant banners from a centre in the sky. Their brightness may vary but during a strong burst of the northern lights, they add considerably to the light from the moon and the stars. At that point, the Arctic light outdoors becomes strong enough to allow you to move about freely at night.

The northern lights are not associated with cold air around us or caused by low temperatures in the air high in the atmosphere. That's a common and understandable misconception, however, because in winter, when the sky is clear and the lights are visible, the air temperature is usually sub-freezing. The northern lights are not seen during the summer simply because its 24-hour daylight is far too intense for these faint lights to be noticeable. The northern

The moon and northern lights illuminate the huge bulk of Iceland's ■ largest volcano, Mt. Öræfajökull (SE Iceland).

■ A fishing vessel is dwarfed by the cone of the Eyjafjallajökull volcano, lit by the winter sun (S Iceland).

lights may be seen in Iceland from roughly the middle of August until the middle of May. But, whether you only want to catch a brief glimpse of such "light entertainment" – or you want to be thoroughly mesmerised by their heavenly, silent show – you must escape from the glare of densely inhabited areas.

Details of the causes and behaviour of the northern lights are still unknown to a certain extent. We still have a great deal to learn about the earth's ionosphere, which interacts with cosmic radiation, the flow of charged atomic particles and flying, interstellar objects. Scientific research on the northern lights has been undertaken by different nations (including Iceland) for decades and Iceland serves as one of the research bases.

THE NORTHERN LIGHTS – WHY?

The violent solar production of nuclear energy, mainly in the forms of light and heat, causes surface phenomena on the sun. Solar flares and incredibly explosive eruptions of glowing hot plasma reaching great heights are among them. So are sunspots, which are large dark-coloured blotches somewhat cooler than the adjoining surface. Sunspots appear at random but have an 11-year cycle of maximum intensity. Solar explosive activity follows sunspot intensity and releases hordes of electrons and protons, which stream into the void. Some of this "solar wind" reaches both the earth's atmosphere and the relatively strong magnetic field that surrounds our globe. This magnetic field attracts and grabs the electrons and protons and sends them spinning toward the surface of the earth. The magnetic force field directs the particles in the direction of the two magnetic poles, close to the true North and South (spinning) Poles. En route, the particles collide with air molecules (mainly oxygen and nitrogen) or single atoms. The energy released by the moving electrons is absorbed by the much larger molecules as well as atoms and is then converted into electromagnetic waves, to be emitted as light. The thin air high up in the ionosphere (70–1,100 km) then starts to "glow" like modern fluorescent light tubes and bulbs. Different colours stem from different energy levels and different molecules. The billowing movement of the northern lights is partly due to the interaction of molecules existing within a limited space and to bursts of electrons entering the atmosphere.

Sunlight colours the ash-filled clouds of a 9 km high eruption column at Grímsvötn, 1998 (Vatnajökull ice cap). ■

VII

Colours in the Sky

Not all sights in the Arctic sky are unique to the high latitudes. This is the case, for example, with rainbows. In Iceland, however, rainbows seem to be more common than in many other countries in the northern hemisphere. Rainbows are hard to count but, if this is true, there are a number of explanations.

In the first place, rainy weather with sunny spells is quite common in Iceland. This provides ideal conditions for rainbows to form. High, interspersed clouds with blustery rain or drizzle speed across the land. From a particular vantage point, the sun may shine between some clouds and pierce others. In such a case, the mass of small raindrops floating and falling in the sky between a spectator and the sun may render a rainbow.

Secondly, many geothermal fields emit steam or fine droplets of water. Given the right conditions, small rainbows form in the steam clouds.

■ A double rainbow is a rare sight.

Thirdly, Iceland is true "waterfall country". Hundreds of large waterfalls line highlands and coastal cliffs. The largest ones, like Dettifoss (44 m high), Gullfoss (34 m high) and Skógafoss (60 m high), carry enough falling water to throw out a large cloud of fine drizzle. Sunny days in Iceland find most waterfalls hosting beautiful rainbow shows.

Rainbows are transient natural phenomena. They disappear as soon as the rain stops or the density of water droplets per volume unit of air drops below a certain level. They are also elusive; if one approaches a rainbow, it moves backward at the same pace the viewer moves forward, and vice versa. The reason for this is found in the very explanation of rainbows: refraction of sunlight in water droplets and reflection of light from them form visible bands of colours at a fixed angle from the sun (or the viewer). If the distance between the moist volume of air and the viewer changes, the four-colour image moves with the viewer. If one is able to stand beneath the end of the rainbow, all wishes come true, so the story goes. Unfortunately, the facts of nature don't support it.

The rainbow is also said to be the Sun King's bow, according to a medieval Icelandic folktale, probably of foreign origin. What would people in the Middle Ages have made of a related but still different phenomenon – the halo? What do we know today? A halo appears high up in the sky as a faintly shining coloured circle around the sun. The halo is usually not composed of the four distinct rainbow colours but made instead of yellowish, faintly reddish bands, some-times even of a brilliant lustre. Commonly, bright spots appear on the ring to the right and left of the sun but sometimes only one is seen on either side of the halo. Ideal weather for halo formation is a thin, wintry cloud cover, with sunshine through the haze. The

Even the sandy deserts and barren mountains of the northeast hold something for ■ the eye. Mt. Herðubreið on the horizon.

■ A rainy day on the black outwash plains of Mýrdalssandur. The Mýrdalsjökull ice cap with the Katla volcano on the horizon (S Iceland).

cloud forms out of minute ice crystals. A halo may appear around a full moon, too, but that is a much rarer sight than an ordinary sun-halo, rare enough in itself.

Halos hold a place in Nordic mythology. According to the Icelandic *Snorra-Edda* manuscript, wolves will engulf both the sun and the moon on Doomsday (at *Ragnarök*). Sköll eats the sun and Hati devours the moon. The two bright spots on the halo (called *úlfur* or "wolf", and *gíll* or "light spot" in Icelandic) were pictured as these two beasts. Furthermore, people believed that the weather would turn bad if only the *gíll* (the spot to the right) appeared. The saying went like this: "Seldom is the bright spot a good sign if the wolf does not follow."

HEAVENLY ARCHES AND CIRCLES

If one regards the sun as a point-like light source, a rainbow appears through a cloud of drizzle or rain as a half-circle at the foot of an imaginary cone. This cone slants at an angle of 84 degrees. Each drop of water in the cloud acts as a common glass prism. The whitish sunlight is bent (refracted) and reflected by billions of droplets in such a way that it breaks into four adjacent circles of the primary colours. At this particular angle from the light source, yellow is at the top and blue (violet) at the bottom. An auxiliary rainbow may form above the main one. If so, the colours appear in the reverse order.

A halo is akin to a rainbow but, instead of water droplets, small ice crystals in a thin cloud refract and reflect the sunlight and produce the halo. The angle of refraction is smaller than in a rainbow. So, a halo commonly forms a whole circle around the sun.

A halo appears above the ice cliffs of the Grímsvötn caldera. The high-altitude ice haze, which helped to create the halo, is ■ the first sign of an advancing low pressure system (Vatnajökull ice cap, SE Iceland).

Warm Iceland

In an oceanic, cool-temperate to mild Arctic climate, good housing is essential. Reliable domestic heating and sufficient light have to be added to the "bare necessities" of life. The Icelanders take care of their heating primarily by utilising their abundant geothermal energy sources. Geothermal areas are found in most regions of Iceland. Hot water or steam wells are produced by drilling boreholes down to a depth of 200–2,000 metres. The raw power of steam is used to generate electric energy or to heat up cold water. Such warmed water flows through pipes and distribution centres to the industrial or domestic user. The majority of wells, however, emit hot water – not steam. And that water, or the above-mentioned steam-heated water, flows through elaborate piping and storage systems to about 90% of all homes and buildings in Iceland. The remaining structures are heated by electricity. Some of the geo-

■ Natural hot springs at Hveravellir on the Kjölur route (central Iceland).

Warm colours and curious cloud formations adorn the surroundings of the Eldborg lava crater (W Iceland)

thermal water provides heat for extensive greenhouse gardening. Artificial lighting speeds up the growth of vegetables and flowers during the dark winter months. Long glasshouses casting a bright, yellow glare stand in stark contrast to white snow.

Most of the electric energy for urban lighting and other uses is produced in hydropower stations built on some of Iceland's many swift rivers. In both cases, by harnessing geothermal energy and hydropower, Icelanders exploit much more environmentally sound methods of energy production than burning carbon fuels or using thermo-nuclear fission.

Light is more than welcome in towns during the winter. Streetlights and glowing signs, patio lights and brightly lit windows keep the impact of darkness to a minimum. In the more sparsely inhabited rural areas, lights are widely dispersed across many lowland areas, reminding travellers and residents of each other's existence and closeness. On the desert-like, coastal sand plains or on highland roads, no house-lights or streetlights intrude upon the darkness.

There are only the occasional headlights of an approaching or passing car. Large highland areas are totally devoid of any artificial lights throughout the winter. Some people find it a ghostly sight.

Lights are used much less in the summer, of course, than in the winter. During the bright summer months, streetlights switch off for up to 24 hours a day. With the sun as a constant companion, the dark, open space of winter under overcast skies, with maybe a single distant light in view, is only a memory. Drivers are, however, required to keep their low-beam headlights switched on throughout the year to make their cars more visible.

The darkest season – that around Christmas and New Year – is strongly illuminated beyond the usual dose of lights. Icelanders' extensive use of coloured lights, candlelight and fireworks must be rooted in a yearning for brightness. In the past, many people were afraid of the dark. Today, the fear is long since subdued by knowledge and by a healthy dose of man-made light.

LIGHT AND ENERGY

Despite Iceland's lack of carbon fuels, it has very large energy resources: namely, the hydropower bound in the rivers and the geothermal energy trapped in the bedrock, heated by the partly molten rock beneath it. Current energy production has only utilised 5–6% of Iceland's geothermal potential and about 14% of its hydropower potential. It is estimated that the technically exploitable hydropower capacity is 64,000 gigawatt-hours (GWh) per year. Some 45,000 GWh are economically exploitable (equal to about 10,000 MW of power), of which the current production capacity is only about 6,350 GWh (about 1,060 MW). An estimate of geothermal energy suggests a technically exploitable capacity of about 125,000 GWh – or twice the hydropower potential. The current exploited capacity is only around 6,500 GWh. Iceland is on its way to becoming the world's first society based on hydropower, geothermal power and hydrogen fuel. The hydrogen will be produced using renewable electric energy and water.

Green and yellow cushions of moss add warmth to the bleak pumice landscape (central Iceland). ∎

Fire from Within

North light is a vaguely defined, non-scientific collection of illumi-
nations and light phenomena in the Arctic. In fact, as a category of
nature, something called "North Light" exists only in this book.
North light is a play on words – but one with potential to end up in
the dictionary.

The rarest and most awesome north light, seen in Iceland and very
few other places in the high north, is the red, orange and yellow
glare from volcanic fire. It is a strange light cast by molten rock, or
magma, which rises from deep within the earth. Volcanic eruptions
occur every fourth year on average in Iceland. Since eruptions and
volcanoes fall into different categories, they radiate different arrays
of light.

■ Explosive activity in the Grímsvötn subglacial volcano, 1998 (Vatnajökull ice cap).

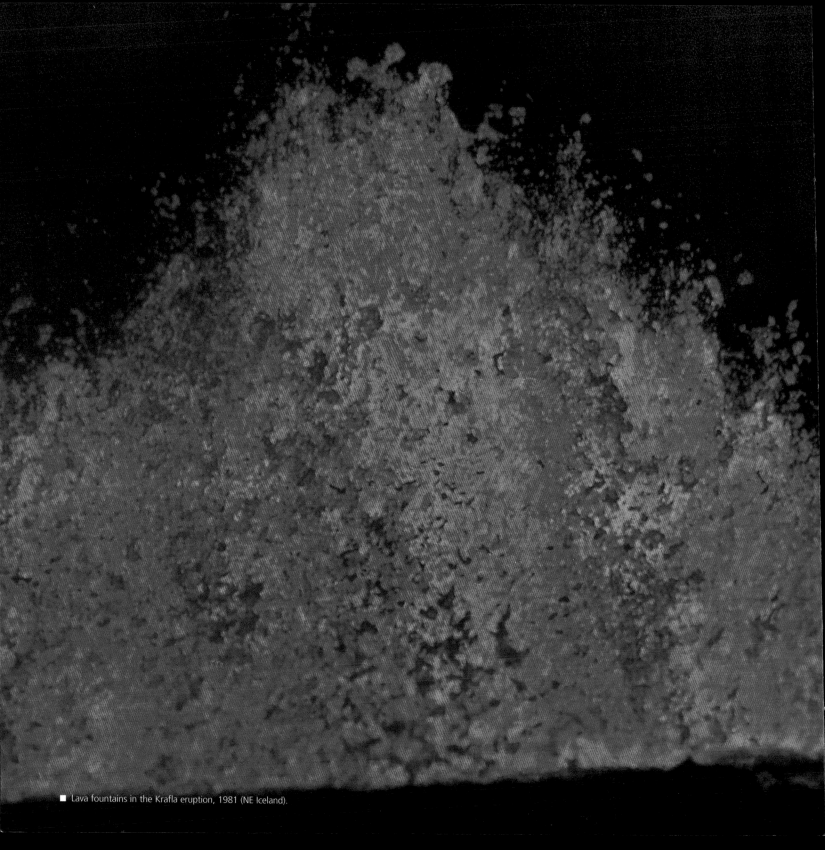

■ Lava fountains in the Krafla eruption, 1981 (NE Iceland).

Iceland's huge central volcanoes are bulky mountains. When they erupt, the eruptives commonly consist both of black, loose material thrown into the air and of flowing lava (1,000–1,130°C). Activity is usually not confined to one crater; fissures commonly open up high on the volcano or lower down on its flanks. Brawling explosions throw a myriad of lava lumps and glowing scoria into the air. Thick, broad rivers of molten rock creep down mountainsides or sweep slopes with lava torrents. When that happens, red to yellow light illuminates the surroundings. Both the sky and large areas around the eruption vents glow restlessly in the dark.

Eruptive fissures open up outside of volcanic centres. Volcanic activity becomes confined to a discontinuous crack in the ground, up to 20–30 km long. Lava fountains form curtains of very hot, fluid lava, breached by explosive activity from time to time. Large streams of lava commonly flow from a row of craters that quickly form along the fissure. These fissure eruptions may illuminate even more of the environment than do the mixed eruptions of the central volcanoes. If the volcanic area has snow cover, its white surface reflects the light and takes on a reddish hue that bathes the landscape in an eerie light. In daytime or during the bright summer season, no light from a volcanic eruption can be seen except by looking directly at lava fountains, glowing lava lumps or the most fluid parts of the lava flows.

Submarine or sub-glacial eruptions glow with no or very little light. The reason is simple: the encounter between water (seawater or melt water from the ice) and magma results in explosions in the water and, consequently, emissions of billowing steam. The main bulk of the eruptives cools very rapidly, disintegrates and turns into

ZONES AND SYSTEMS

Contrary to common belief, the crust cannot split open just anywhere in Iceland and start to spout lava or pumice. The present rift zone and two volcanic flank zones form the active volcanic zone of Iceland, and volcanic activity is confined to those particular parts of the country. In most of the regions outside this zone – to the east and west – the earthly fires have been absent for hundreds of thousands or even millions of years since these regions drifted away from magma sources. The area of the active volcanic zone is 25,000 sq km or about a fourth of Iceland. Within the zone, volcanoes and volcanic fissures don't appear at random, but are confined within elongated areas characterised by fissures, faults and volcanic formations. These areas are termed "volcanic systems" and most are 5–20 km wide and 20–150 km long. There are about 30 volcanic systems in Iceland, including hundreds of volcanoes. Three systems are on the Snæfellsnes Peninsula, four on the Reykjanesskagi Peninsula, six in south Iceland, four in northeast Iceland and the remaining fourteen dot the central highlands. Many volcanic systems are partly or wholly covered by ice caps and the highest volcanic cones (stratovolcanoes) are all glaciated. In coastal areas and in the lowlands, a number of volcanic systems cut into townships or inhabited rural areas.

Mt. Hekla during the January 2000 eruption (S Iceland). ■

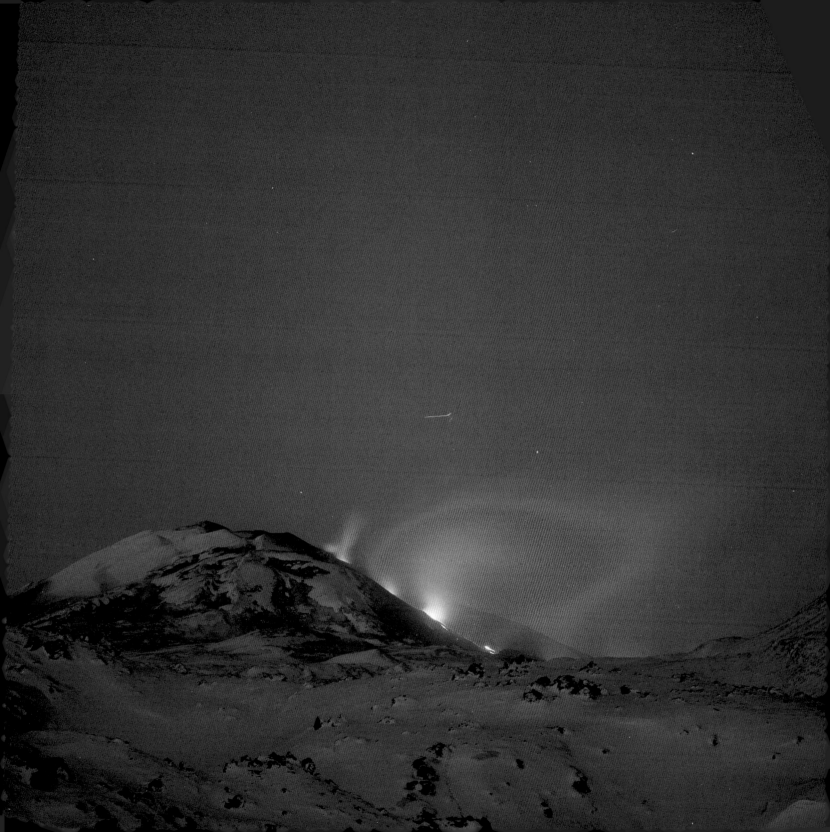

black ejecta (called tephra), thrown high into the air. No sound booms are heard. A hissing noise is more common. A few glimpses of glowing magma may add an eerie glow to the black ejecta.

Occasionally, conditions for lightning activity ripen in the rising cloud of steam and gases above the volcano. Then, dozens of lightning bolts are visible at once, illuminating both the cloud column and the sky. Thunder echoes and could be mistaken for explosions. In sunny weather, any rising eruption cloud takes on various colours according to its tephra content, as well as the position of the sun. When the sun shines through such a cloud, colours of gold appear and the evening sun paints the clouds with orange and violet shades.

BORN AND BRED BY FIRE

Over the past 18–20 million years, combined magma production of the normal up-flow at the Icelandic rift zone – along with magma from the Iceland hot spot (mantle plume) – managed to build a more than 200,000 sq km platform of lava fields and other magmatic rocks in Icelandic waters. Almost half of it is a shallow-sea platform; the rest constitutes the present island, sometimes rising 1,000–2,000 m above sea level. Some 50% of the dry land area rises to at least 400 m above sea level. Iceland began to form in the late Tertiary period as a much smaller volcanic island or group of volcanic islands, and has since grown into a sizable island (103,000 sq km). In Iceland, as in other parts of the world, erosion and weathering counteract tectonic uplifting and volcanic build-up to some extent. Iceland is probably no longer growing in size – or at least not very quickly, because of the sculpting processes. But the distance between the towns of Ólafsvík in the West and Seyðisfjörður in the east is growing steadily, by 2 cm per year on average, due to the tectonic processes of plate spreading.

Born and bred by fire... These gentlemen skateboarders are waiting for the last evening bus in the July twilight. ■

Just Wait and See...

A visitor to Iceland may hear a worn-out joke about the weather. It goes like this: "If you don't like the weather at the moment, just wait five minutes." The joke has its foundation in the sudden and frequent shifts in Iceland's weather. The explanation for the shifts is found in at least three factors: the location of the island in the North Atlantic Ocean at a relatively high latitude, a high-profile landscape, and the paths of low-pressure systems from the southwest to the northeast across the ocean.

The weather systems either pass very close to – or directly over – Iceland. As they approach, southerly winds prevail. But as soon as they've passed, the wind usually turns into cooler northerlies. Blowing from the ocean, the stronger winds usually carry clouds

■ The turn of the millennium was celebrated by firework displays above the old harbour in Reykjavík.

and precipitation to whichever side of Iceland they reach first. Meanwhile, on the other side (leeside), the resultant dry air simultaneously leads to much sunnier weather (the föhn-effect). The weather systems commonly travel quickly, so changes come in rapid succession. To be an Icelander is to be engaged in a never-ending dance with the weather. And you have to dance fast. Calm and generally stable weather prevails if no prominent "lows" are close to Iceland, if a "high" has built up over the island, or if "lows" pass far to the south of Iceland. Such conditions sometimes last up to two weeks, much to the joy of the Icelanders (and their many visitors).

The weather casts its spell on all walks of life and, of course, on nature. The landscape takes on a new look for each weather-type; and even these types can vary within themselves. During periods of showers, the sun shines for a short period and is then blocked by fast-moving clouds, only to shine again. Sunbeams, dark and bright contrasts, dispersed sunlight... they all pique the imagination. Such differentiating light gives birth to a new landscape with the coming of every moment. Clear weather in the winter with the sun low on the horizon lends the landscape an extraordinary sharpness and, occasionally, a diamond-like glittering of snow and ice. Different

THE SEA IS THE KEY

The warm oceanic Gulf Stream from the Caribbean has an enormous impact on Iceland's temperatures and weather. This current transports warm seawater to the Arctic Circle. In general, the Icelandic lowlands have a mild to cool oceanic climate while the highlands are characterised by a somewhat sterner – but still relatively mild – polar climate. At this latitude on the continents, temperatures are generally much colder in the winter and warmer in the summer than they are in Iceland. Winter conditions in Iceland, however, can often turn extreme when very high winds or churning blizzards make an air temperature of only -5 to -15°C bite like an Arctic wolf. They remind you of your latitude. While it often rains on Christmas Eve in Reykjavík, this rarely happens in the north of Iceland. About 20% of the annual precipitation falls as snow in the southern lowlands while the figure is 50–60% in the northern lowlands and valleys.

In towns such as Reykjavík and Akureyri, rain (or snow) is certainly not too abundant but periodic showers or a few hours of continuous rain or snow from a passing front are quite common. Days with precipitation number 212 per year in Reykjavík and 139 in Akureyri. Looking on the bright side, it's good to know that the average annual hours of sunshine in Iceland range for example from 1,200 hours in Reykjavík to 1,000 hours in Akureyri.

So, Iceland may not be the sunniest place in the world but at least the weather is very seldom dull!

Hauling fish to shore and processing it has long been the mainstay of the Icelandic economy. However, it is not always an easy task. ■

■ Sheep grazing amid blazing autumn colours (W Iceland).

■ Reflected sunlight in rain clouds off the south coast. The Vatnajökull ice cap in the background (S Iceland).

shades of grey and white during heavy rain or fog enshroud everything with a dull atmosphere and a tint of mystery. A blizzard paints everything white and the late evening sun turns the world of Iceland orange.

Air pollution is uncommon in Iceland. Chemical smog is absent, except over Reykjavík on a very calm day. In the case of hazy weather, the somewhat restricted visibility is usually the result of natural water vapour in the air, pollution carried by the wind from mainland Europe or fine-grained soil particles from soil erosion

areas within Iceland. Visibility in Iceland is generally excellent. The cone-shaped Snæfellsjökull central volcano is, for example, a common sight from Reykjavík – 110 km distant across the bay of Faxaflói.

This is why the weather is indeed a challenge for the senses and why Icelanders aren't only dependent on the weather in an economic sense but also for a stimulating, annoying or joyful partner. To the photographer, the shifting weather in Iceland turns out to be an interesting challenge, to say the least.

Nature as a master of the abstract (the shore of Lake Kleifarvatn, SW Iceland). ■

North Light
Text © Ari Trausti Guðmundsson 2002
Assistance with English text: Mike Handley
Photos © Ragnar Th. Sigurðsson 2002
Design: Erlingur Páll Ingvarsson

First published in 2002 by Iceland Review ©,
an imprint of Edda Media & Publishing,
Reykjavík, Iceland.
Printed in Iceland.

ISBN 9979-51-189-3

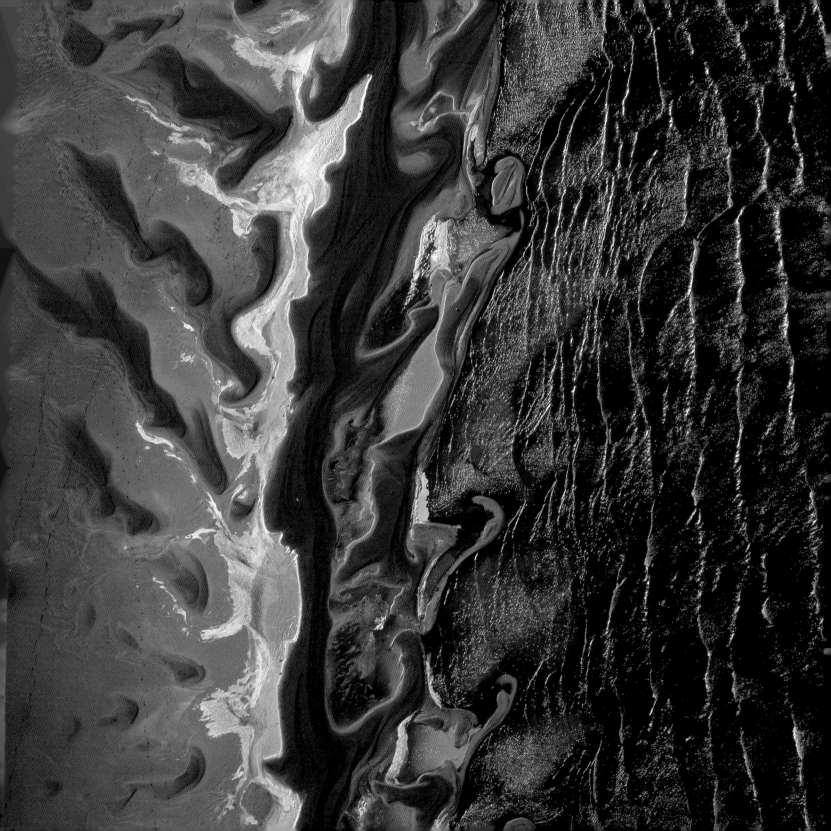